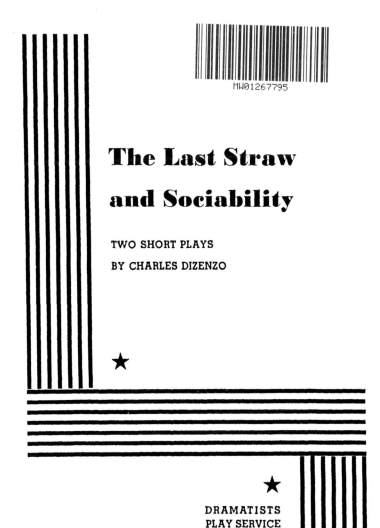

MW01267795

The Last Straw
and Sociability

TWO SHORT PLAYS
BY CHARLES DIZENZO

★

★

DRAMATISTS
PLAY SERVICE
INC.

ABOUT THE AUTHOR

Mr. Dizenzo grew up in Hackensack, New Jersey. He got his B.A. at New York University and did time at Massachusetts Institute of Technology, N.Y.U. School of Law and Georgetown University School of Medicine.

The Last Straw was first presented at The American Place Theatre in March, 1970. The previous season his plays *A Great Career* and *An Evening for Merlin Finch* were presented at Lincoln Center's Forum Theatre and at Belgrade Theatre, Coventry, England. *An Evening for Merlin Finch* was also chosen by The Repertory Theatre of Lincoln Center for its Theatre-in-the-Schools program, and a separate production of the play was seen by 100,000 high school students in the New York metropolitan area. It was the first new play to tour under this program.

In New York, his plays have also been produced by The New Dramatists Committee, The Barr-Albee Playwrights' Unit, Theatre Genesis of St. Mark's Church, Theatre for Ideas, and Channel 13's New York Television Theatre. David Merrick presented his play *Why I Went Crazy* at Westport Country Playhouse and Falmouth Playhouse, Cape Cod.

Mr. Dizenzo spent a year writing at Yale ('66-'67) under a Yale-ABC Fellowship and received a Guggenheim Fellowship for playwriting the following year. He and his wife, also a writer, live in Manhattan.

Dramatists Play Service publishes other one-act plays by Mr. Dizenzo: *The Drapes Come*, *A Great Career*, and *An Evening for Merlin Finch*. Dramatists Play Service also handles amateur rights for his play *Big Mother* and furnishes the Grove Press edition of this play.

3

THE LAST STRAW

A COMEDY IN ONE ACT

By Charles Dizenzo

THE LAST STRAW was first presented by The American Place Theatre, in New York City, in March 1970. It was directed by Gregory C. Meland; the scenery and costumes were by Kert Lundell; and the lighting was by Roger Morgan. The cast, in order of appearance, was as follows:

DOCTOR FRANK .... Edward Kovens

ANTHONY .... Oliver Clark

CAST OF CHARACTERS

DR. FRANK—*A middle-aged man, older than forty-five, younger than sixty-five.*

ANTHONY—*A young man, older than seventeen, younger than twenty-seven.*

6

THE LAST STRAW

A junky one-room office with beat-up desk and chairs, old file cabinet, desk lamp and coat rack. The office is virtually bare but for these.

Dr. Frank, a middle-aged man slovenly dressed in out-dated business clothes, sits behind his desk. He is playing solitaire.

There is a knock on the door.

Dr. Frank pauses, then gathers his cards together and puts them in his desk.

DR. FRANK. (*Calling out.*) One minute, please! I'm on the phone. . . . (*He takes the phone off the hook, lays the receiver on the desk, gets up, pushes his shirt into his pants, saunters over to the door, arranging his tie and jacket as he goes. Opening the door, pleasantly.*) . . . Come in, please. (*Anthony appears at the door. He is a young man in his early or mid-twenties, earnest and, at the moment, uneasy.*)

ANTHONY. I'd like to see Doctor Frank.

DR. FRANK. (*Cheerily.*) Come in, please.

ANTHONY. Are *you* Doctor Frank?

DR. FRANK. (*Proudly.*) I am *the* Doctor Frank.

ANTHONY. (*An embarrassed smile.*) May I see you professionally?

DR. FRANK. Please come in.

ANTHONY. (*Entering, looking around shyly, struck by the seediness of the place, slightly appalled.*) Is this your office?

DR. FRANK. (*Defending his dignity.*) For the moment. It's my temporary office.

ANTHONY. (*A nervous, winning smile.*) May I sit down?

DR. FRANK. Please do.

ANTHONY. Thanks. . . . (*He walks over to the desk, looking the place over, turns around a few times in doing so, and winds up sitting in the Doctor's seat behind the desk. Dr. Frank gives him a cold stare.*) . . . Is something wrong?

DR. FRANK. You're sitting in my seat.

ANTHONY. (*Getting up fast.*) Sorry. Where shall I sit?—There?
DR. FRANK. Sit down, please.
ANTHONY. Thank you. . . . (*Sitting in the visitor's chair. Dr. Frank takes his seat behind the desk.*) . . . Well, I read your ad. . . . (*Dr. Frank just looks at him.*) . . . Well, I read it—and here I am. . . . (*Dr. Frank just stares.*) . . . I want to do something about myself, about my whole life-style.
DR. FRANK. One minute, please. I'm on the phone.—An ex-pupil. (*Picking up the receiver, which has been lying on the desk and pretending to hold a conversation.*) Sorry, Girard; a visitor. You were describing how my course changed your life. (*Pause.*) You're happy now? (*Pause.*) Successful in your work? (*Pause.*) Very successful? (*Pause.*) Advancing rapidly, showing initiative. (*Pause.*) A new promotion and a big raise? (*Pause.*) The boss likes you. Your co-workers like you.—Everybody likes you, is that right? (*Pause.*) You're happily married, but you also have other women. Ah, Girard, I knew you could do it. (*Pause.*) I see: Now you're dynamic, handsome, vital, well-off, well-groomed, a good public speaker, tell good jokes, you're a swinger, write good business letters, a good physique, inspire trust, handy around the house, a regular stud, own two cars, repair your own radios, read twice as fast with more comprehension, a black belt in judo, play golf, have charisma and good table manners, active in community affairs, master of Chinese checkers, no more shyness, no more homosexuality, no more depression, no more bad breath, no more loneliness, no more feelings of failure. Well, Girard, sounds like you're quite a new man. Glad you took my course? (*Pause.*) Very glad, right? Well, so long, Girard. Keep in touch. (*Hangs up, to Anthony, rather unnecessarily.*) That was Girard, an ex-pupil. Doing very well now.
ANTHONY. (*Looking around, nervously.*) I thought you'd have a different kind of office.
DR. FRANK. I told you it's temporary. Moving to larger quarters.
ANTHONY. Where's your staff?
DR. FRANK. On vacation. We move to the Time-Life building next month. What is your complaint?
ANTHONY. About the office?
DR. FRANK. (*Impatiently, but still smiling.*) What brings you here?
ANTHONY. (*Rattled, uncomfortable.*) Oh; well, I'm dissatisfied

with myself; I'm dissatisfied with my life. (*With sudden urgency, leaning toward the Doctor.*) Do you really think you can do something about it?

DR. FRANK. Describe yourself.

ANTHONY. (*Reflectively, earnestly.*) Well, I'd say I'm the mild-mannered Clark Kent type. I'm shy with strangers, I tend to bumble, I blush easily—but inside me I feel there's a Superman.

DR. FRANK. Are you married? Do you work?

ANTHONY. (*Apologetically.*) I'm not married, but I do work. I used to work for a newspaper as a matter of fact. (*Pause.*) I was fired.

DR. FRANK. And now?

ANTHONY. (*Sourly.*) It's office time.

DR. FRANK. You work in an office?—Where?

ANTHONY. I'd rather not say. If they knew I was here I'd be persona non grata.

DR. FRANK. Anything you tell me is confidential.

ANTHONY. (*Uncomfortably.*) Sure, but anything I *don't* tell you is *really* confidential.

DR. FRANK. Are you always so mistrustful?

ANTHONY. Let's just say I work in Manhattan.

DR. FRANK. If you want my help I must know *more* about you.

ANTHONY. Doctor, are you a Ph.D. or an M.D.?

DR. FRANK. (*Proudly.*) I'm Ph.D. *and* M.D.

ANTHONY. (*Resigned.*) Well, what do you have to know?

DR. FRANK. What are your symptons?

ANTHONY. You mean physical symptoms? I've got every symptom, Doctor. You name it, and I'll claim it.

DR. FRANK. List them.

ANTHONY. (*Cheerfully businesslike.*) My pleasure: Lower-back pain, insomnia, constipation, migraine headaches—I've got one now, Doctor, a killer—I over-perspire, short breath, diarrhea—two r's—all I ever want to do is sleep, flat feet, cancer—just kidding, Doctor—compulsive eating with no appetite, a constant lump in my throat, I cry at the drop of a hat, I laugh with no provocation, I'm completely passive—total ennui, Doctor, I couldn't care less—and yet I can't sit still for five minutes. Do you have an aspirin?

DR. FRANK. (*Shouting angrily for no apparent reason.*) No aspirin!

ANTHONY. (*Confused.*) No aspirin?

9

DR. FRANK. (*Calm again.*) What are your aspirations?

ANTHONY. I want to be happy in the worst way.

DR. FRANK. What are your aptitudes?

ANTHONY. I don't have any.

DR. FRANK. Surely you have *one*.

ANTHONY. No, I don't have any.

DR. FRANK. Do you have any hobbies?

ANTHONY. Well, I used to collect coins, foreign coins, when I was small, but I'm not interested in coins any more. It's fine for kids. They learn a lot of geography from it. But it's a waste of time for somebody my age.

DR. FRANK. What do you collect now?

ANTHONY. Nothing. I gave up collecting altogether.

DR. FRANK. (*Solemnly.*) Rash! Very rash.—Any other hobbies?

ANTHONY. I read a lot, if that's a hobby.

DR. FRANK. (*Irritably.*) That's not a hobby. What about interests? Are you interested in anything?

ANTHONY. Well, I'm interested in drama and film art.

DR. FRANK. (*Annoyed.*) Film art?

ANTHONY. You know, movies.

DR. FRANK. (*Disgusted.*) Plays and movies. You're interested in them, eh?

ANTHONY. Yes, and I have some pretty strong views about the direction they should move in.

DR. FRANK. (*Disgusted.*) You do, eh?

ANTHONY. And as I said, I'm interested in reading, especially modern literature. . . . (*Dr. Frank remains silent, looking disgusted.*) . . . And then Dance is pretty interesting. Except it's so non-verbal. . . . (*Dr. Frank looks really disgusted now.*) . . . And probably Art is interesting too. You know, fine art. Painting and sculpture and everything. Except that's not very verbal either. . . . (*Dr. Frank is starting to get really annoyed.*) . . . But sometimes they use words in their paintings now and bits of newspaper and stuff. . . . (*Dr. Frank is hard put to keep his irritation under control.*) . . . Picasso does that. Mostly French words. Because he's Spanish, I guess. . . .

DR. FRANK. (*Very irritated.*) That's enough about your interests. How long have you been suffering?

ANTHONY. It's been a progressive thing, Doctor. These last months have been awful.

DR. FRANK. And before that?

ANTHONY. Before that things were awful.

DR. FRANK. And before that?

ANTHONY. Awful!

DR. FRANK. And before that?

ANTHONY. Awful! Things have been awful for a long time, Doctor. I just never noticed it.

DR. FRANK. (Reprovingly.) It's high time.

ANTHONY. The scales dropped from my eyes, Doctor. I've been living in a fool's paradise. Now I see my life, even life in general, the way it really is, and it's just awful!

DR. FRANK. (Disgusted.) So you want to be happy!

ANTHONY. (A bit frenzied, relieved that somebody presumably understands.) You see my arm, the way it's attached to me? I can move it up, move it down, move it out, bend it, but I can't get rid of it! (Getting up, very excited.) And my legs, Doctor; I move away, and they run under me. I make a quick turn, they follow! I jump, but they grab on and drag me down!—Inescapable ballast! My head sits on my neck getting a free ride everywhere! I move it, shake it, swing it, but it's on my neck for keeps—for life— forever! (Sitting down again, depressed.)

DR. FRANK. (Blasé.) How long have you been bored?

ANTHONY. (Calm again.) I've been bored for five and a half years.

DR. FRANK. (Conclusively.) That's malaise.

ANTHONY. (Relieved and excited that he understands.) That's it, Doctor. That's me.

DR. FRANK. Torpidity. You couldn't care less.

ANTHONY. That's it, Doctor. You've really nailed it down!

DR. FRANK. I can cure it.

ANTHONY. (Elated; jumping up; a big smile.) You can? You can cure it? (Approaching the Doctor.) Oh, Doctor, are you sure? (Moving around the desk.) You're not just bragging? You really mean it?

DR. FRANK. (Uncomfortably.) Please sit down.

ANTHONY. (Moving behind the desk and hugging the Doctor.) Oh, my little Doctor! (Giving him several warm kisses.) My own little Doctor!

DR. FRANK. (Struggling to extricate himself from Anthony's

11

grateful embrace.) Please, now please! No physical contact! Sit down!

ANTHONY. (*Subdued, returning to his seat, gratefully.*) Well, certainly, Doctor. You're in charge here. How long before I'm cured? How long before I'm happy?

DR. FRANK. Half an hour.

ANTHONY. (*Delighted.*) Half an hour! That's marvelous! I thought it'd take much longer!—like months or something!

DR. FRANK. I can cure you this afternoon. (*Going to closet.*)

ANTHONY. (*Delighted.*) You mean I'll be happy tonight? Oh, my god, I'm delighted! It's been so long, I've almost forgotten what happiness feels like! I wonder if I'll recognize it, maybe have a little Proustian moment, remember the taste of a cookie I once ate or something. . . . (*Dr. Frank takes out a headpiece with strange electrical wires. It should have a dilapidated look, very much like it's been constructed out of miscellaneous old junk found in an appliance repair shop. Anthony, still not seeing the headpiece, babbling on happily.*) . . . A new life-style for Anthony! I'll buy all new clothes, clothes with a little dash! A blazer, maybe a red vest! I'd hate to change too much, though. I'm very used to me as I am. I don't want to me too cured. (*Spotting the headpiece.*) —You don't expect me to put that on, do you?

DR. FRANK. (*Winningly.*) I put it on your head.

ANTHONY. (*Worried.*) What is it?

DR. FRANK. Patent pending.

ANTHONY. What does it do?

DR. FRANK. (*Reasonably.*) Put it on your head.

ANTHONY. How does it work?—Is it electrified?

DR. FRANK. (*Trying to lower it on his head.*) Put it on your head.

ANTHONY. (*Stopping him.*) Now wait a minute!

DR. FRANK. (*Angrily.*) Put it on your head!

ANTHONY. (*Standing up.*) How does it work? What does it do?

DR. FRANK. Sit down!

ANTHONY. (*Sheepishly sitting down again, Dr. Frank starts to lower it onto his head.*) Wait a minute! (*Trying to stop him again.*)

DR. FRANK. Shut up!

ANTHONY. (*Covering his head with his arms.*) Wait a minute! I want to know what it does! I'm not touching it until I know what it does!

12

DR. FRANK. (*Angrily, imperiously.*) What's your name?

ANTHONY. (*Still seated, huddling down with arms over head.*) Anthony.

DR. FRANK. (*Calmer, setting down the headpiece on the desk.*) So, Anthony, you want to know what it does.

ANTHONY. (*Resentfully.*) Well, it's *my* head.

DR. FRANK. (*Sitting down, patiently, fatherly, kindly.*) I'll tell you what it does. In layman's terms, it scrambles your head and makes it come out right.

ANTHONY. (*Abruptly demanding.*) Do you have a license?

DR. FRANK. (*Irritated.*) A license?

ANTHONY. (*Aggressively.*) Do you have a practicing license? Are you registered?

DR. FRANK. (*Insulted, angry.*) Registered? Do you think I'm a dog? Do you want me to wear a tag?

ANTHONY. You *don't* have a license, do you?

DR. FRANK. (*Angrily defending himself.*) I have all the credentials!—Plus degrees, plus personal endorsements; plus famous testimonials, verified and authenticated!

ANTHONY. (*Defiantly suspicious.*) *What* degrees?

DR. FRANK. Berlin, Buenos Aires, Lyons, Vienna, Bologna, New School, Heidelberg, and Prague! I am well trained, highly competent and highly dedicated! I want you to get well quick! You're afraid of this apparatus!

ANTHONY. (*Suspicious, defiant.*) Shock therapy?

DR. FRANK. No! You don't know anything! (*Pointing to headpiece.*) This is negative reinforcement. I show you slides and zing you a little, and that's all.

ANTHONY. That's shock therapy!

DR. FRANK. No! Electrotherapy, D.C. only. It zings, and that's all.

ANTHONY. (*Getting up.*) It's too expensive.

DR. FRANK. There's no fee.

ANTHONY. Why not? Doesn't it work?

DR. FRANK. It works one hundred percent.

ANTHONY. (*Defiantly, trying to show him up.*) Why isn't there a fee?

DR. FRANK. (*Ignoring the question, restating his main argument.*) There is absolutely no charge.

ANTHONY. (*Starting to leave.*) I don't like this set-up.

DR. FRANK. (*Commandingly.*) Sit down right now! Pay me *after* treatment. Pay me what you like. Pay me nothing! Sit down! (*Anthony, despite himself, finds himself sitting down again, completely intimidated.*)

ANTHONY. (*Bitterly.*) I just hope you know what you're doing. (*Dr. Frank plunks the headpiece down on his head, pulls a strap under his chin and starts to lock the strap in place with a key. Anthony, alarmed.*) Is that a lock?

DR. FRANK. I lock it on your head. (*Plugging the apparatus into an electrical socket.*)

ANTHONY. (*Irritably.*) Now what's the point of that?

DR. FRANK. (*Scornfully.*) What do you think the point is? The point is you can't get it off your head— (*Dr. Frank flips on a slide projector. The slides are not seen by the audience. The actors look out at the audience as though the slides are projected there.*) All right, now, describe the slide, please.

ANTHONY. (*Bored.*) It's a naked woman.

DR. FRANK. Correct. Good. Say "good."

ANTHONY. (*Bored.*) Good.

DR. FRANK. (*Changing the slide.*) All right, describe the slide.

ANTHONY. (*Bored.*) A naked man. (*Dr. Frank pulls a lever. The bulb on his headpiece lights up, a buzzer buzzes, and Anthony howls in pain.*) Aaaaaaaah!

DR. FRANK. Bad. Say "bad."

ANTHONY. Bad! (*Dr. Frank pulls back the lever, and the buzzer and lights are killed. Anthony, outraged.*) What *is* this?

DR. FRANK. (*Changing slides.*) Describe the slide.

ANTHONY. A lady's breast.

DR. FRANK. Good. Say "good."

ANTHONY. What *is* this?

DR. FRANK. Look at the slide and say "good."

ANTHONY. Good.

DR. FRANK. (*Changing the slide.*) Describe the slide.

ANTHONY. (*Looking at the slide in surprise.*) What *is* this?

DR. FRANK. Describe the slide.

ANTHONY. (*Irritated.*) A man's prick. . . . . . Aaaaaaah! (*Dr. Frank again throws the switch.*)

DR. FRANK. Bad. Say "bad."

ANTHONY. Bad! (*Dr. Frank cuts off the juice. Anthony, furious:*) Now, listen!

DR. FRANK. (*Changing slides.*) Describe the slide.

ANTHONY. It looks like a human anus. . . . Now, listen, . . . Aaaaaaaaah! (*Dr. Frank has again thrown the switch.*)

DR. FRANK. Bad. Say "bad."

ANTHONY. Bad! (*Dr. Frank cuts off the juice.*)

DR. FRANK. (*Changing slides.*) Describe the slide.

ANTHONY. Take this off my head.

DR. FRANK. Describe the slide.

ANTHONY. Unlock me!

DR. FRANK. Do as I say or I'll zing you.

ANTHONY. (*Reluctantly looking at the slide, angrily.*) It's sex!

DR. FRANK. What kind?

ANTHONY. The bad kind! (*He jumps up and leaps for the plug. Dr. Frank throws the switch. The lights and buzzer go off, and Anthony reels around, tethered by the plugged cord, in frenzied pain, howling.*) Aaaaaaaaaaaaaah! (*Anthony and Dr. Frank grapple as Dr. Frank tries to block his way to the switch and plug. Finally Anthony reaches the plug and pulls it out. He sinks into Dr. Frank's desk chair overcome with exhaustion and relief.*)

DR. FRANK. (*After a pause, observing him, sullen and disappointed.*) The treatment's not over.

ANTHONY. You shut up.

DR. FRANK. You're a long way from happiness.

ANTHONY. Shut up! (*Pause, resentfully accusing.*) That was for homosexuals, wasn't it?

DR. FRANK. All purpose.

ANTHONY. (*Furiously.*) Well, I'm not a homosexual!

DR. FRANK. Defensive?

ANTHONY. Brilliant diagnosis, Doctor—Where's the key?

DR. FRANK. You got scared, am I right?

ANTHONY. (*Fooling with his headpiece, trying vainly to get it off.*) Where's the key, you quack?

DR. FRANK. (*Angrily.*) To stop now isn't good! You came to me for help. You came to me with questions. You came to me for happiness and answers. Unfortunately you're a physical coward. Unfortunately you're paranoid. You want to leave and never come back. If you leave you will remain a nonentity. You'll always be a colorless spittle-licking nothing!

ANTHONY. (*Looking foolish, the apparatus still on his head, angrily.*) Who's colorless?

15

DR. FRANK. (*The tirade continues.*) You're afraid of life; you're afraid of happiness. But you have great capacities, you have untapped potential, you have personality, looks, talent, everything—but you don't want to admit it! Now admit it!—What is your sign? When were you born?

ANTHONY. (*Morosely.*) I'm a Gemini.

DR. FRANK. (*Pretending to be impressed and delighted.*) Gemini!—Very good! What's your birth date?

ANTHONY. May twenty-first.

DR. FRANK. The twenty-first!—Very good! A first-decan Gemini. . . . (*There is a trace of his having learned this by rote and of his repeating this from a book verbatim.*) You combine stability, a keen sense of logic, and a desire for justice. You have an excellent memory and unquenchable curiosity. Your mind is analytic and clever.—Isn't that so?

ANTHONY. (*Still morose, but fast becoming friendly.*) What if it is?

DR. FRANK. You have a deep sense of personal responsibility, think objectively and clearly, but unfortunately tend to restrict your range of opinions through lack of self-confidence.—Correct?

ANTHONY. (*Less morose, but a bit depressed.*) It's true.

DR. FRANK. We can fix that. Your great drawback is restlessness. In your eagerness for action you fail to set a goal. To develop your highly charged personality you must accept conventions and an orderly way of life.

ANTHONY. (*Just catching on, distressed.*) Astrology?

DR. FRANK. Your quick mind gives you great advantage in the legal profession. Your clever hands insure success as a dentist or surgeon. Many Geminians are electricians, printers, and engravers. —What do *you* do?

ANTHONY. (*Disappointed, resentful.*) I told you: I work in an office. (*Pause, bitterly.*) And I don't believe in astrology!

DR. FRANK. Now, listen, your problem is inhibition. I can help you open up. There is a series of exercises that unleash sexuality forever. Your body comes alive and *stays* alive. Take off your shirt.

ANTHONY. Please, Dr. Frank.

DR. FRANK. No apparatus. This method makes you sexual. A new vitality fills you. Sexual potency returns and stays. You get fast promotions. Take off your shirt.

ANTHONY. Is this a physical?

DR. FRANK. No.

ANTHONY. Then what is it?

DR. FRANK. Neo-Reichian, amended by me. Take off your shirt.

ANTHONY. (*Starting to take off his shirt.*) Neo what? What is this?

DR. FRANK. Take off your shirt and pants. Please keep your underwear *on.*

ANTHONY. (*Peevishly, taking off his shirt.*) Well, that's for sure.—What's this do?

DR. FRANK. For neuro-muscular relaxation, removing inhibitions, making you sexually free.

ANTHONY. (*Interested.*) No kidding?

DR. FRANK. Take your pants off.

ANTHONY. Does it work? Have you tried it before?

DR. FRANK. Foolproof. It's yet to fail. Take off your pants.

ANTHONY. I'm going to.

DR. FRANK. You're taking forever. That's repression.

ANTHONY. I can go just so fast.

DR. FRANK. Soon you'll find clothes come off faster; no more jammed zippers.

ANTHONY. Nothing's jammed. I'm going as fast as I can.

DR. FRANK. Energy begins to flow faster; life becomes joyous.

ANTHONY. (*Taking off his pants, hopefully.*) And no more malaise, right?

DR. FRANK. Right! Complete sexual liberation. Lift your arms over your head, elbows straight.

ANTHONY. (*Taking his pants off.*) Wait a minute.

DR. FRANK. No more anxiety. No more boredom. You sleep like a log, and you can't wait to get up.—Extend arms over head.

ANTHONY. Okay, . . . (*Dropping pants in chair.*) . . . Extend arms over head.—Is this it?

DR. FRANK. Please, up on your toes.

ANTHONY. (*Confused.*) What is this?—Ballet?

DR. FRANK. Now, stretch. Stretch up, extend yourself up, high as you can go, move against gravity, soar above yourself. Stretch your neck up, stretch your fingers, even your nails; try to touch heaven itself.

ANTHONY. (*Doing it, but confused.*) What's this for?

DR. FRANK. It works one hundred percent.

ANTHONY. What's it *do?*

17

DR. FRANK. Lower arms parallel to floor. Describe a circle with your wrists.

ANTHONY. What?

DR. FRANK. Wave your arms at your sides; make circles.

ANTHONY. Like this?

DR. FRANK. Faster. Stretching. Faster.

ANTHONY. All right?

DR. FRANK. Faster. Much faster.

ANTHONY. (*Confused.*) I'm gonna take off.

DR. FRANK. Please, faster!

ANTHONY. (*Waving his arms.*) What's going on? What's happening?

DR. FRANK. Now, staying on toes, arms on hips, please joggle.

ANTHONY. Joggle?—What are you talking about?

DR. FRANK. Joggle, jog, prance like a donkey.

ANTHONY. A donkey?—What do you think I am?

DR. FRANK. No questions.

ANTHONY. (*Prancing on his toes in silence for a while.*) Well?— Now what?

DR. FRANK. Keep joggling.

ANTHONY. (*Keeping it up.*) What good can this do?

DR. FRANK. No questions. Do what you're told.

ANTHONY. (*After prancing in silence for a while.*) Dr. Frank, I'm getting tired.

DR. FRANK. No talking.

ANTHONY. (*Prancing, annoyed.*) No talking? (*Prancing in silence.*) Dr. Frank, I'm ready to drop! (*Prancing in silence, finally stopping, exhausted, huffing and puffing.*) I've had it, Dr. Frank. That's it.

DR. FRANK. (*Sharply.*) Wait! What are you doing?

ANTHONY. (*Starting to put on his pants.*) I'm getting dressed.

DR. FRANK. Keep them off.

ANTHONY. (*Pleading, angrily.*) I'm freezing!

DR. FRANK. I forbid it!

ANTHONY. (*Putting on his pants, muttering.*) I've humored you long enough.— (*Angrily.*) I'm not catching pneumonia!

DR. FRANK. Don't worry about pneumonia.

ANTHONY. (*Getting dressed.*) Thanks for the free treatment.— (*Bitterly.*) I'm sure it's done me lots of good!

DR. FRANK. I absolutely forbid you to dress!

18

ANTHONY. (*His pants are on now, reaching for his shirt.*) What kind of crackpot are you?

DR. FRANK. (*Angrily grabbing Anthony's shirt off the chair.*) Remain where you are!

ANTHONY. (*Trying to grab his shirt away from Dr. Frank.*) Give me that!

DR. FRANK. (*Holding on to the shirt.*) I forbid you to touch it!

ANTHONY. (*Angrily yanking at it, a tug of war ensues.*) You do, huh?

DR. FRANK. (*Holding on to one end.*) I forbid you to disobey!

ANTHONY. Oh, you do! (*Yanking the shirt out of the Doctor's hand with all his might.*) For a weak old bird you do an awful lot of forbidding. (*Examining the shirt, outraged.*) You wrinkled it! This was a fresh shirt!—Now look at it! It's all wrinkled!

DR. FRANK. (*Scornfully.*) Of no consequence.

ANTHONY. You old buzzard! It's of consequence to *me*.

DR. FRANK. Petty bourgeois nonsense.

ANTHONY. (*Putting on his shirt.*) I ought to make you pay to get it ironed.

DR. FRANK. Take it from my fee.

ANTHONY. (*Angrily.*) Fee?—You're not getting a penny.

DR. FRANK. Standard fee!

ANTHONY. Nothing!—That's your fee!

DR. FRANK. Standard rates!

ANTHONY. (*Buttoning his shirt.*) You're getting a big zero.

DR. FRANK. Services rendered!

ANTHONY. (*Tucking in his shirt.*) You old buzzard.

DR. FRANK. (*Reprovingly.*) No names!

ANTHONY. You're a fraud!

DR. FRANK. (*Outraged.*) Names!

ANTHONY. (*Putting on his jacket.*) You're a quack!

DR. FRANK. (*Horrified.*) Names!—Bad names! . . . (*Faking an attack, sinking in his chair, holding his chest.*) . . . Names! . . . . Aaaaah . . . . Aaaaah . . . . Aaaaaaaaaah!

ANTHONY. (*Putting on his jacket, irritably.*) What's eating you?

DR. FRANK. My chest. . . . Aaaaaaah!

ANTHONY. (*Going over to him, progressively alarmed.*) What's wrong? Is it something you ate? Are you in pain? Don't you feel well?

DR. FRANK. (*Pretending to have a hard time getting up.*) Names,

19

bad names! Aaaaaah! My medicine! . . . (*Collapsing on the floor in front of his desk while trying to reach the file cabinet.*) . . . Aaaaaah!

ANTHONY. (*Kneeling down next to him.*) Oh, my god, what's wrong with you?

DR. FRANK. My medicine! Get it at once!

ANTHONY. (*Getting up, running to desk.*) Oh, my god, sure, . . . (*Ransacking the desk drawers.*) . . . Sure, no trouble at all. Where's it at? I can't find it!

DR. FRANK. (*Lying on the floor, moaning dramatically.*) Idiot!— In the file!

ANTHONY. Oh, my god, . . . Where's the file? . . . Oh, . . . (*Running to the file and ransacking it.*) . . . I can't . . . Where? . . . What's it filed under?

DR. FRANK. Idiot!

ANTHONY. (*His hackles up.*) Now wait a minute!

DR. FRANK. (*Clutching his heart.*) Aaaaah!

ANTHONY. (*Forgetting his grievance, ransacking the file.*) Oh, my god! . . .

DR. FRANK. Bottom drawer!

ANTHONY. (*Inspecting the bottom drawer.*) There's nothing here but aspirin.

DR. FRANK. That's it.

ANTHONY. (*Surprised.*) Aspirin?—I thought you said you didn't have any.

DR. FRANK. Aaaaah!

ANTHONY. (*Handing him aspirin.*) Here. Come on, open up. Dr. Frank, come on, open up. (*Getting down on his knees to hand it to Dr. Frank.*) Maybe you should take two.

DR. FRANK. Only one.

ANTHONY. Y'sure? (*Getting up and starting for the phone.*) I'll call a doctor.

DR. FRANK. (*Grabbing his leg.*) No! No doctors!

ANTHONY. (*Trying to keep him quiet.*) Maybe you should just lie there.

DR. FRANK. (*Getting up slowly.*) Not necessary.

ANTHONY. Shouldn't you lie quiet for a while?

DR. FRANK. (*Trying to get to his feet, using Anthony for support.*) Help me.

ANTHONY. Please, I really think you should lie where you are.

DR. FRANK. Pull me.

ANTHONY. (*Pulling him up.*) What happened?—Some kind of awful attack? (*Getting a chair and placing it near Dr. Frank.*) I was so scared I practically died.—Was it your heart? I nearly passed out. (*Using Anthony's support, Dr. Frank sits down in the chair. Anthony, uneasily.*) Comfortable now? How do you feel?—Better? How do you feel?—Like a new man? I better be going.

DR. FRANK. (*Grabbing his arm.*) No!

ANTHONY. (*Dying to get out, but trying to be polite.*) I'd like to stay, but, . . .

DR. FRANK. No! Treatment isn't done. Another method.

ANTHONY. (*A big phoney smile, uncomfortably.*) But you already cured me.—Honest!

DR. FRANK. Not true, not yet.

ANTHONY. (*With phoney cheerfulness.*) I really do feel better.—Happy!—And you did it, Doctor.

DR. FRANK. No, a different method.—Talk therapy. You talk, and I listen.

ANTHONY. Please, Dr. Frank.

DR. FRANK. Psycho method. You talk and talk, and I do nothing. Works one hundred percent.

ANTHONY. You should think about your *own* health.

DR. FRANK. Tell me something awful about your childhood.

ANTHONY. I don't like to talk about it.

DR. FRANK. Even better. Tell me something terrible.

ANTHONY. Nothing terrible happened.

DR. FRANK. Something embarrassing.

ANTHONY. Nothing happened. I was four, then I was five, then I was six, and that's about it.

DR. FRANK. How did you pass the time? Did you play baseball?

ANTHONY. (*Matter-of-factly.*) My sport was killing ants. (*Uncomfortably.*) I used to step on them.

DR. FRANK. Elaborate a little, but not too much.

ANTHONY. There's nothing much to say. There were some ant holes in the grass by the sidewalk in front of our house, and they'd cross the sidewalk to get to the other side, as they say, and I'd step on them. I didn't want them using the sidewalk.

DR. FRANK. Why not?

ANTHONY. I don't remember. It's been years now. But it used to infuriate me. I'd see one edging toward the pavement, and I'd wait

21

quietly until he'd crawled to the middle of the concrete, and . . .
(*Leaping and stamping down his foot.*) Bam! I'd squash him. Then
maybe I'd turn around and another ant would be making a dash
for it. . . . (*Wheeling around and stamping his foot.*) Bam! . . .
I'd nail him. The hard part would be when maybe a half dozen
ants would make a break for it in different spots at the same time.
(*Wheeling around and stamping on imaginary ants.*) Bam! . . .
Bam! . . . Bam! . . . Bam! . . . Bam! . . . Bam! (*Depressed.*)
They never learned. I guess they're not too bright.
DR. FRANK. Why did you do that?
ANTHONY. (*Ruefully.*) I don't know. But I always buried them.
Every ant in a separate grave. I had an ant cemetery in the back-
yard. I'd poke a little hole in the ground, put in a dead ant, cover
it up, and stick in a little cross made of toothpicks. . . . (*Laugh-
ing.*) It was the biggest ant cemetery in the country.
DR. FRANK. (*Aghast.*) This is really sick.
ANTHONY. (*Defending himself.*) They asked for it!
DR. FRANK. Shows a disturbed personality. Don't do it any
more.
ANTHONY. I don't.
DR. FRANK. When you see an ant, turn the other way.
ANTHONY. I gave up ants with foreign coins.
DR. FRANK. You wanted to murder your mother and father. You
wanted to squash them like bugs.
ANTHONY. (*Bored and annoyed.*) Oh, please.
DR. FRANK. You hated them for having sex and leaving you out.
ANTHONY. (*Acting bored, put off.*) Shows what you know:
They don't *have* sex.
DR. FRANK. (*Knowingly.*) You *wish!*
ANTHONY. They don't. They don't enjoy it.
DR. FRANK. They conceived *you,* didn't they?
ANTHONY. They had relations once or twice, and that was it.
DR. FRANK. Wishful thinking.
ANTHONY. (*Pretending to be bored.*) Please, this is getting too
personal.
DR. FRANK. Why do you object to your parents having sex?—
The truth!
ANTHONY. (*Getting up.*) Listen, this is ridiculous.
DR. FRANK. For all you know, they're having sex right now!

ANTHONY. (*Starting for the door, annoyed and a little worried.*) I'm going home.

DR. FRANK. Leave them in peace.

ANTHONY. (*Angrily.*) I'm going to my home; I don't live with them.

DR. FRANK. I don't believe you.

ANTHONY. That's your problem.

DR. FRANK. You're lying! You don't want them having sex!

ANTHONY. (*With hard-won calm.*) If it makes them happy, I'm all for it.

DR. FRANK. (*Shouting in his face.*) It *does* make them happy, and they're fornicating right now!

ANTHONY. (*Pushing him.*) What do *you* know, you old fart! You don't know anything. (*Marching toward the door.*)

DR. FRANK. Face facts! For once in your life face reality! (*Whipping a cloth off a concealed object on his desk to reveal a crystal ball.*) Look for yourself! Go on, I dare you to look!

ANTHONY. (*Turning back at the door.*) A crystal ball? . . . (*Curiosity gets the better of him, and he moves back to the desk.*) . . . Well, that's the limit, you fraud. . . . That's the last straw.

DR. FRANK. You're grasping at straws.

ANTHONY. (*Looking into the crystal ball.*) I don't see anything. (*Starting for the door again.*)

DR. FRANK. (*Pointing.*) Look more carefully.

ANTHONY. (*Looking again.*) There's nothing in there.

DR. FRANK. Open your eyes! Focus!

ANTHONY. Where?

DR. FRANK. Look closely— There in the middle.

ANTHONY. That shadow? That light?—It's a reflection!

DR. FRANK. It's an *image.* You see that dark spot?

ANTHONY. There?

DR. FRANK. It's your father's pecker!

ANTHONY. (*Shoving the Doctor.*) You dirty old creep! It's glass! It's a phoney! You're full of it! (*Starting for the door.*)

DR. FRANK. (*Grabbing him by the wrist.*) One minute!

ANTHONY. Let go, you old quack!

DR. FRANK. (*Holding on.*) Give me!

ANTHONY. (*Trying to shake off the Doctor's grip on his arm.*) I said hands off! (*Yanking his arm, he causes Dr. Frank to fall down; the Doctor is still gripping his wrist.*)

23

DR. FRANK. (*Examining his palm, pretending alarm.*) Oh, my god! Your hand! The lines! Your line of life!—You're going to die!

ANTHONY. More bullshit!

DR. FRANK. (*Pointing out lines on Anthony's palm.*) You're going to die young! Your line of destiny!—You're going to fail in everything you try and then die young!

ANTHONY. (*Trying unsuccessfully to yank his hand away.*) Bullshit!

DR. FRANK. Look! Look at that short line. That's the girdle of Venus. See where it stops? It means you'll never know love.

ANTHONY. (*Yanking his hand away and hitting the Doctor.*) I'm reporting you, you goddam quack! What do *you* know? Look at you! Look at you! You're a broken-down old nut!

DR. FRANK. (*Outraged.*) Incurable! Incorrigible! Doomed!

ANTHONY. (*Heading for the door.*) You crazy old half-assed crackpot! I hope you die!

DR. FRANK. (*Agonized, an attack—fake or real—coming on.*) Quack! Fraud! Buzzard! Phoney-baloney! Murdered with insults! Aaaah! (*Holding his heart.*)

ANTHONY. (*Opening the door, hesitating.*) What are you doing?—Having another fake attack?

DR. FRANK. My medicine!

ANTHONY. You're the boy who cried-wolf.

DR. FRANK. You selfish swine! You pig! Leaving me to die like a dog! I curse you! Die! Die like a pig, you dog!

ANTHONY. Goodbye forever, you goddam quack! (*Exiting.*)

DR. FRANK. (*Moving to door.*) Come back here! Come back here! Come back . . . (*Lights fade out on the Doctor, who is seen returning to his desk, dejected, in the fading light. Anthony returns from the wings with a lighted cigarette. A spotlight catches him as the lights die out on the Doctor.*)

ANTHONY. (*Reflectively and amiably to the audience.*) I never went back; but I know Dr. Frank recovered because his ad kept appearing in the papers: (*Using a radio announcer's tone for the ad.*) "Are you lonely? Are you alienated? Do you feel like you're visiting an alien planet? Are your friends beginning to act like alien beings?—Visit Dr. Frank." (*The usual tone.*) It was a good ad; it used a lot of stuff from science fiction movies— You know the kind of movie. (*Using a deep super-rational voice.*) "Joe, you're my best friend. I'm beginning to worry a little about Francine. She's been acting strange lately, sort of vague and distant. Do you think her body's been invaded by an alien being?— Here she comes; don't say anything.—Hey, Francine, what's new?" (*Now acting Francine, using the stock science fiction movie sound effect for alien beings, a high, piercing trill, arms stretched forward robot-style.*) "Li-li-li-li-li-li-li-li-li-li-li-li." (*Using the deep rational movie voice again.*) "See what I mean, Joe?—Her mind! Her mind!"— (*Returning to initial usual tone.*) —As for Dr. Frank, in a strange way he helped me. I was desperate when I showed up at his place, grasping at straws, any kind of solution. My life was a bunch of questions and no answers. When he finished with me I figured there *weren't* any answers. So, I did the only thing there *was* to do.—I picked myself up and went on.

END OF PLAY

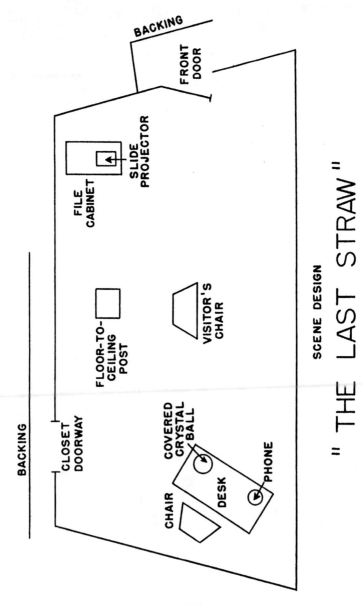

SCENE DESIGN

" THE LAST STRAW "

PROPERTY PLOT

On Stage:
  Beat-up desk. On it:
    Deck of cards
    Desk lamp
    Telephone
    Crystal ball (covered)
  Chairs
  Old file cabinet. In it:
    Aspirin
  Coat rack
  Slide projector
  In closet:
    Headpiece, with wires

Off Stage:
  Cigarette (Anthony)

Personal:
  Key for lock on chin strap of headpiece (Dr. Frank)

SOCIABILITY

A COMEDY OF MANNERS IN ONE ACT

By Charles Dizenzo

CAST OF CHARACTERS

Fanny and Frank .... *Wife and husband*

Milly and Jack .... *Wife and husband*

The four characters should be in the same age range. The range itself can vary from early thirties to early fifties. Perhaps forty is best.

NOTE TO READER

This play is written to be played at the pace of leisurely conversation, with plenty of breathing space for pausing, thinking, and silent reaction. Since the lines are short and simple, the play can be read very quickly; but the reader ought to slow down to the rate of slow conversation to get the feel of the play.

Also, the four characters, despite the unlikeable things they say and do, are meant to be played "likeable." I've added "happily" and "cheerfully" as stage directions to every other line, and the reader should supply them even where I haven't.

SOCIABILITY

The set should look like a sketch of a living room. Except for sofa, coffee table, and two easy chairs, all the other furnishings can be painted on the backdrop.
Fanny and Frank, a married couple, occupy the room. Their age can range anywhere from thirty to fifty-five, though perhaps around forty is best.

FANNY. (*Cheerfully.*) Frank, I don't mean to be pedantic, but they were supposed to be here at eight.
FRANK. Maybe something detained them.
FANNY. Well, they should call and admit it. This is a case of bad manners.
FRANK. They'll come. I think you'll like them.
FANNY. What's Jack like?
FRANK. (*Cheerfully.*) Jack's a sort of a hot-shot go-getter who's going nowhere fast.
FANNY. Is his wife nice?
FRANK. Well, Jack describes her as a sort of a quiet, mousy loud-mouth with a lot of free time on her hands. She sounds a lot like you.
FANNY. Some couple. Why'd you ask them here?
FRANK. Well, Jack sauntered over during a coffee break, expressed an interest in seeing us socially and inspecting our home, and I couldn't say no.
FANNY. (*Cheerfully.*) I would've.
FRANK. Fanny, I promise if you act really vivacious we won't see them again. That's a promise, Fanny. (*The doorbell rings.*)
FANNY. (*Rising, vivaciously.*) I guess that's them. Do I look my best? I want to look good for our new friends.
FRANK. Relax. They'll love you. (*Opening the door.*) Well, if it isn't Jack! (*Jack and Milly enter. They are a married couple about the same age as Frank and Fanny.*)
JACK. (*Happily.*) Well, look who's here!—It's Frank! Sorry we're late. Something detained us.

31

FRANK. (*To Fanny, happily.*) See?—Didn't I tell you? Fanny, this is Jack from the office and probably his wife.

JACK. That's her.—It's Milly. Milly, this is Frank from the office and Fanny, right?

FANNY. (*Happily.*) Right! Well, this is a real pleasure.

MILLY. (*Happily to Fanny.*) I haven't heard anything about you, but it really seems like I have.

FANNY. (*Happily to Milly.*) Haven't we met before?

MILLY. You know, I just met you, and already I like you?

FANNY. Well, come in and sit on something. (*Pointing to sofa.*) This looks comfortable. Try it on.

MILLY. It *does* look comfortable! (*Sitting.*) Oh, it *is!*

JACK. (*Happily to Frank.*) You know, you look just like you do at work, only more so.

FRANK. (*Happily.*) I'd recognize you anywhere.

JACK. You know, I like you at the office, but here I *really* like you.

FRANK. (*Happily.*) Aw, go on!

JACK. No, I mean it!

FANNY. (*To all, happily.*) I suppose you want some drinks.

JACK. Right!

FANNY. Milly, can I get you a drink?

MILLY. (*Happily.*) Is there anything to eat?

FANNY. (*Happily.*) No.

MILLY. (*Happily.*) Some peanuts or something?

FANNY. (*Happily.*) No, nothing. Jack, will you join the festivities?

JACK. (*Happily.*) Right!

FANNY. (*Happily.*) What do you want, Frank?—Something?

FRANK. (*Happily.*) Yeah, make it something.

FANNY. (*Happily.*) I suppose I have to *fix* the drinks, right?

FRANK. (*Happily.*) Right! Why don't *you* fix them?

FANNY. (*Happily.*) As usual, the pleasure's all mine. (*Starting to fix drinks at a little portable bar.*)

MILLY. (*Happily.*) What a charming place for a home!

FRANK. (*Happily.*) *We* like it.

MILLY. Oh, you could do wonders with this place!

JACK. (*Happily.*) It's a lot like ours before we fixed it up.

MILLY. (*Happily.*) You should have *seen* our place before we worked it over.—It was nothing to speak of.

JACK. I've got photos to prove it. It looked a lot like this place, only better.

FRANK. (*Happily.*) Is that right?

FANNY. Here's your drink, Milly. Hope you enjoy it.

MILLY. It looks delicious. (*Taking a sip.*)

FANNY. Enjoying it?

MILLY. (*Happily.*) I sure am!

FANNY. (*Happily.*) Wonderful! Here's yours, Jack.

JACK. (*Happily.*) Thank you, Fanny. (*Holding it.*)

FANNY. (*Happily.*) Go on, have a sip.

JACK. (*Putting down the drink, happily.*) I'd rather wait a second.

FANNY. (*Happily.*) Have a sip now, Jack.

JACK. (*Sipping the drink.*) Wonderful!

FANNY. (*Happily.*) Glad you're enjoying it.

JACK. (*To Frank.*) Say, if you don't mind telling, how much did you pay for this place?

MILLY. Jack!

JACK. (*Happily.*) How much? Was it much?

FRANK. (*Happily.*) How much was yours?

JACK. About thirty-five thousand.

FRANK. (*Happily.*) That's what we paid.

JACK. (*Surprised, happy.*) That much?

MILLY. (*Sipping her drink, happily.*) Well, I like it here. I like the atmosphere.

FANNY. (*Happily.*) Thank you, Milly. Have another sip. (*Pause, happily.*) Go on, have one!

MILLY. (*Happily taking another sip.*) Fanny, you're the hostess with the mostest.

JACK. (*Happily.*) Of course, with the renovations we made, our place actually cost more. Thirty-five thousand for the place and fifteen thousand for renovations, making a grand total of fifty thousand.

MILLY. (*Happily.*) You'll love our place!

JACK. You've got to come over and see it.

FANNY. (*Happily.*) It sounds too far away.

MILLY. It's really very near.

FANNY. (*Happily.*) Well, that's a matter of opinion.

MILLY. It's just around the corner.

FANNY. (*Cheerfully.*) Sorry, it's too far.

JACK. It's just a stone's throw from here.

FANNY. (*Happily.*) You hear that, Frank?

MILLY. You walk out that door, go straight until you hit the sidewalk, turn left, walk to the corner, and it's the third house on your left.

FANNY. That's quite a trip!

MILLY. (*Happily.*) It's not that far.

JACK. We walked it.

MILLY. We're walking home too.

JACK. We left both cars home and we walked!

MILLY. We've got two cars.

JACK. If you don't want to walk over, we could pick you up. (*To Frank.*) I could pick you up . . . (*To Fanny.*) And Milly could pick you up.

FRANK. (*Cheerfully.*) We've got our own cars.

MILLY. Do I understand that you have *two* cars?

JACK. That's right.

MILLY. (*Happily.*) Well, you could take one, and Fanny could take one, or you could both come together.

JACK. Or I could pick up one of you, and the other could drive over in one of *your* cars.

MILLY. Whatever's convenient.

JACK. (*Cheerfully.*) How much do your cars cost?

FRANK. One cost four thousand, and one cost two thousand.

JACK. What could you get for them now?

FRANK. I could get two thousand for one and five hundred for the other.

JACK. (*Cheerfully.*) Oh, come in *our* cars.

MILLY. Whatever's convenient.

FRANK. I could get three thousand for one and one thousand for the other.

FANNY. (*Cheerfully.*) I'd rather walk or not come at all.

MILLY. Whatever's convenient.

FRANK. (*Happily.*) It's getting late, isn't it?

MILLY. Not really.

FRANK. Well, since you're walking home, you should start early.

MILLY. But we just live around the corner.

FANNY. (*They've made no move to leave, happily.*) Going so soon?

MILLY. (*Getting up, happily.*) I'm afraid we've got to be going.

FANNY. (*Happily, protesting.*) But, . . .

34

MILLY. (*Happily.*) Now, now, don't try and dissuade us. When we make up our minds, you can't budge us.

JACK. (*Getting up, an independent thought.*) I think we should go.

FANNY. (*Cheerfully.*) Well, it's been something meeting you, Jack.

JACK. (*Happily.*) Let's get out of here.

MILLY. Let's do this again some time at *our* place.—You'll love it!

FANNY. (*Happily.*) Milly, it's really been something.

FRANK. (*Happily.*) Goodbye.

JACK. Let's go.

MILLY. (*At the door.*) I don't know which of you I like best.

FANNY. I hope it's me.

MILLY. (*Cheerfully.*) I don't think so.

JACK. (*Exiting.*) Bye.

FRANK. See you at the office.

MILLY. (*Exiting.*) So long now!

FANNY. (*Cheerfully.*) Bye! (*Closing door behind them, happily.*) I like them.

BLACKOUT

Lights up on the same living room set, only now Milly and Jack occupy it. It is their home.

MILLY. (*Anxiously.*) Do you think they'll like our home?

JACK. Why shouldn't they like it?

MILLY. (*Looking around worriedly.*) Does it look all right? How's the atmosphere?

JACK. I feel right at home.

MILLY. Now you act relaxed, and I'll be cordial, and I think things'll be fiine. (*The doorbell rings, getting up to answer the door.*) Do I look casual? Yes? Good. (*Opening door, happily.*) Well, look who we've been expecting! It's them!

FANNY. (*Entering cheerfully.*) I hope we're not early; we came on time.

FRANK. We brought both cars.

MILLY. (*Cheerfully.*) You shouldn't have!

JACK. (*Happily.*) Who drove which?

35

FRANK. I drove the new one—which I got yesterday.

FANNY. (*Happily.*) Shall we all take a ride in it?

MILLY. (*Happily excited.*) How exciting!—Let's stay here!

FRANK. (*To Jack.*) I think you'll like it. It cost five thousand dollars.

JACK. (*Happily.*) That's more than mine cost!

FRANK. (*Cheerfully.*) I'll say.

JACK. (*Happily.*) But I *make* more than you.

FRANK. You *used* to. I got a raise.

MILLY. Look at our lovely home! Isn't it nice?

FRANK. I'm making two thousand more now.

MILLY. Like our home? It's completely renovated.

JACK. I'm due for a raise soon myself. I'll be making four thousand more.

FANNY. Any refreshments?

MILLY. (*Cheerfully.*) Of course there's refreshments. Why not sit down first?

FANNY. Wonderful!

MILLY. You want a nice chair or a nice sofa?

FANNY. I want some nice refreshments.

MILLY. Why don't you try our new sofa? It cost a thousand dollars.

FANNY. Sounds wonderful! (*Sitting down.*)

FRANK. (*Cheerfully.*) When are you getting the raise?

JACK. It should be pretty soon.

FANNY. (*Happily.*) *How* soon?

FRANK. You might not get that raise.

FANNY. (*Cheerfully.*) Was it actually promised to you?

FRANK. (*Cheerfully.*) Lots of times they tell you you *might* get a raise, but then you don't get it.

MILLY. (*Happily.*) He's getting it.

FANNY. (*Happily.*) He might not *get* it.

MILLY. What about refreshments? We always serve them here.

FANNY. (*Happily.*) I'm famished! Do they taste good?

MILLY. I make them myself.

FANNY. (*Happily.*) Well, I'm famished; I'll have some.

FRANK. I'll take a lot.

JACK. What about some drink?

FRANK. Count me in!

FANNY. Wonderful!

MILLY. (*Exiting to kitchen.*) To sum it up, I'll get the refreshments . . . (*To Jack.*) . . . You do the drinks, and then we'll all rest and have an interesting conversation.

JACK. (*Making drinks at portable bar.*) Do you like our home?

FANNY. Wonderful!

JACK. Do you like me and Milly?

FANNY. Wonderful!

JACK. Are you glad you came?

FANNY. Are we ever!

MILLY. (*Entering with pie, plates, etc.*) Here we are! Home-grown pie, made the real way!

FRANK. Hey, that smells great!

MILLY. Now, while I cut it, you be saying something interesting.

FANNY. There's a local bakery that makes a really delicious pie. You go in there, give them money, and they give you a pie that's wonderful!

MILLY. (*Giving her a piece of pie.*) Here, Fanny. You've got a real treat in store for you.

FANNY. This looks like something! (*Talking and eating.*) The pie at that bakery has a flake so crusty you want to melt it in your own mouth. And the pie filling, which they also invent on the premises, is real fruit, freshly picked and pitted that very day!

MILLY. (*After giving pieces to Frank, Jack, and herself, to Fanny, cheerfully.*) Enjoying my pie?

FANNY. (*Happily, a delighted discovery.*) This tastes a little like the pie I'm talking about!

MILLY. (*Taking away her plate on which there is still plenty of pie.*) Finished? Let me take your plate. Goodbye. Enjoy the drive home. (*Helping Fanny and Jack up out of their seats and moving them toward the door.*)

FRANK. I hate to leave so soon, but I've got work tomorrow, and with my new salary I shouldn't be late for the office. (*Milly pushes them out and slams the door shut.*)

BLACKOUT

Lights go up on the same set, but now it is Fanny and Frank in their living room.
The doorbell rings.

FRANK. (*Rising to answer it.*) If that's them I'll tell them you died or something.

FANNY. If that's them I *will* die. (*Frank opens the door. Milly and Jack barge in. Milly is carrying a bakery box.*)

MILLY. Surprise! It's us! Surprised to see us? We dropped over on the spur of the moment!

JACK. It was spontaneous.

MILLY. (*Holding out bakery box.*) I got you three dollars from your favorite bakery.

FANNY. (*Delighted.*) Milly, what did you just say?

MILLY. (*Cheerfully.*) I got you three dollars from your favorite bakery!

FANNY. (*Delighted.*) Oh, Milly, you shouldn't have!

MILLY. I wanted to *do* it!

FANNY. Three dollars! I love it!

MILLY. (*Happily.*) Now don't make a fuss! It only *cost* three dollars. They were fresh out of four dollars, and I knew that next to four dollars, you like three dollars best.

FANNY. You always get what we nearly like best! (*Admiring Milly's coat.*) My, what an expensive coat you're having!

MILLY. (*Happily.*) It cost three hundred dollars.

JACK. (*Happily.*) My coat cost two hundred dollars

MILLY. (*Substitute "lovely" for "seventy-dollar" for right intonation.*) Isn't that a seventy-dollar hostess outfit!

FANNY. (*Cheerfully.*) Thank you! Are you going home now?

MILLY. (*Happily.*) No, we're staying.

JACK. It's a celebration.

MILLY. Jack got a new salary today.

JACK. (*A happy smile.*) Higher than yours. (*A cheerful grin to Frank.*) Much higher.

FANNY. (*Happily reaching for Milly's coat.*) May I take your three hundred dollars?

MILLY. To hang up while we're here?—Wonderful!

JACK. (*Still smiling cheerfully at Frank, pointing at him.*) Much higher than yours.

FANNY. Jack, can I take your wrap?

JACK. I'll say.

FANNY. (*Pointing to chair and sofa.*) Why don't you sit on something expensive? Milly, you sit here on five hundred dollars; and, Jack, you sit on fifteen hundred dollars over there.

JACK. (*Happily.*) Doesn't look like fifteen hundred to me.

FANNY. (*Cheerfully.*) What's that, Jack?

JACK. (*Happily.*) I said you can tell it has value.

FANNY. (*Giddily.*) It should: It cost fifteen hundred dollars. (*Exiting.*) I'm going out in the kitchen and divide this three dollars by four—Seventy-five cents each.

JACK. Did I mention I got a raise today?

FRANK. Yes.

JACK. (*As though he said "no."*) Well, I got a raise. A real biggie.

MILLY. Three thousand dollars.

FRANK. How's it feel to be making three thousand more a year, Jack?

JACK. Well, I'll tell you, Frank, it makes me feel worth about three thousand more a year.

FRANK. (*Happily.*) As much as that!

JACK. Maybe more!

FRANK. (*Cheerfully to Milly.*) I'm due for a new salary soon myself.— (*Nodding toward Jack.*) And he might get fired.

MILLY. (*Happily.*) That'll be the day.

FANNY. (*Returning with the cake.*) Well, here we are, returning with dessert!

MILLY. Fanny, the three dollars looks delicious!

FANNY. Will everybody join me in a cup of small change? I'm brewing a pot.

MILLY. Wonderful!

FANNY. It's the kind served to the help at the Waldorf Astoria. I think you'll like it. (*Exiting.*)

FRANK. (*Cheerfully.*) Don't tell anybody, but I heard a rumor you might get fired.

JACK. (*Happily.*) It's strictly a rumor.

FRANK. I hear it's gonna happen. (*Fanny returns with coffee pot, cups, sugar bowl and creamer on a tray.*)

FANNY. (*Setting down tray.*) Well, here I am, folks, returning with small change. Milly, you'll have a dime, won't you?

MILLY. (*Taking cup and saucer from her.*) D'love it!

FANNY. (*To Jack, cheerfully.*) Jack-ass?

JACK. You bet!

FANNY. (*To Frank.*) Frankly?

FRANK. I'll say!

FANNY. (*Passing around bowl and creamer.*) Now who wants pennies?

JACK. Me.

MILLY. I do.

FANNY. (*Happily.*) Now let's have a conversation.

FRANK. We just had a conversation.—Let's play bridge.

MILLY. (*An independent brainstorm.*) Say! Why not play bridge!

JACK. Great idea!

FANNY. Wonderful!

FRANK. (*Happily.*) Wish I'd thought of it.

FANNY. (*Going to sideboard.*). I'll get our two-dollar deck.

FRANK. (*Exiting.*) I'll get our sixty-dollar table and chairs.

MILLY. This chair is so comfortable I think I'm going to have an orgasm.

JACK. (*Interested.*) No kidding?

FANNY. (*Returning with cards.*) It *is* a comfortable chair. It cost five hundred smackers.

MILLY. I've never felt anything quite like it.

FANNY. Shall we play a penny a point, just to make it interesting?

MILLY. A penny a point?

FANNY. To make it more exciting.

FRANK. (*Setting up chairs and table.*) To keep us awake.

FANNY. To make it more fascinating.

JACK. Best idea I've heard all week!

FANNY. Come on, everybody, sit over here.

MILLY. I really hate to leave this chair behind.

FANNY. I know what you mean.

MILLY. (*Rising.*) I've never been felt by anything quite like it.

FANNY. Five hundred. Come on, Milly, you deal.

MILLY. (*Dealing cards out.*) One for you, one for you, one for you, one for me. One for you, one for you, one for you, one for me. . . .

BLACKOUT

Lights go up on the same scene, the four of them around the bridge table.

FRANK. (*Rising, cheerily.*) Okay, that's it, get up, the game's over.

MILLY. (*Happily.*) Who won?

JACK. (*Cheerily.*) They did. We're the guests, and they won.

MILLY. I hated that game.

FRANK. Okay, go home.

JACK. Who wants to stay longer?—Not me!

FANNY. (*Cheerily.*) Go home now. I've had about enough of this.

JACK. (*Happily.*) A tremendously boring evening, Frank; it was great!

FANNY. (*Enthusiastically.*) Let's cut this short, all right? I want to sleep off this whole experience.

JACK. Who wants to stay longer?—Not me?

MILLY. (*Happily.*) Likewise, I'm sure, Fanny. (*Seeing the window curtains.*) Fanny! You got new curtains and you never mentioned them!

FANNY. (*Yawning, happily.*) It's getting to be about that time, Milly.

MILLY. (*Going over to the curtains.*) What beautiful curtains! I love them! (*Ripping down a curtain, rod and all.*)

FANNY. (*Patiently, trying to remain cheerful.*) Glad you like the curtains.

MILLY. (*Bringing the curtain forward to Fanny.*) Fanny, this is a wonderful curtain! Speaking frankly, it looked ugly up there, but down here it's wonderful! Will you feel the material?

FANNY. I felt it.

MILLY. Some strong material! What is it—fiberglass?

FANNY. Rayon.

MILLY. Is it dacron?

FANNY. Nylon.

MILLY. Is it orlon?

FANNY. Banlon.

MILLY. Some strong material! It really wears! (*She rips the curtain in half.*)

FANNY. That curtain was twenty dollars.

JACK. (*Moving toward a vase.*) What's this?—A vase?

FRANK. Fifty dollars.

41

JACK. I like it. (*Hurling the vase to the floor where it shatters.*) Too bad about that vase. It was darned attractive.

FANNY. That vase was an heirloom.

JACK. I don't like vases; but that vase I liked.

MILLY. Fanny! What a striking lamp!

FANNY. Like it?

MILLY. I'm stricken with it! Can I stroke it?

FANNY. Rather you didn't.

MILLY. I'm really struck with it! (*Picking it up.*) I practically worship this lamp! (*Throwing it to the floor where it breaks.*) Was that an heirloom too?

FANNY. That lamp was priceless.

FRANK. It cost eighty dollars.

FANNY. That lamp was struck.

JACK. Good work, Milly.

MILLY. Thanks, Jack. Fanny, dear, is that a new dress?

FANNY. Seventy dollars.

MILLY. Lovely! Lovely workmanship! (*Ripping the dress off Fanny's back.*)

JACK. (*To Frank.*) Nice suit. (*Ripping Frank's jacket in half off his back, then ripping off his trousers.*)

FRANK. (*Standing in his underwear.*) It cost a hundred and twenty dollars.

FANNY. (*Sweetly.*) Okay, go home now. Ripping is the last straw.

MILLY. (*Pointing to Fanny's shredded dress.*) But I like the dress.

FRANK. (*Opening the front door for Milly and Frank to leave, cheerily.*) Time to go.

JACK. Why the big change in attitude?

FANNY. (*Cheerily.*) It's no fun being with you.

FRANK. Fanny's got a point. We don't want to be friends any more.

JACK. You've got us all wrong.

MILLY. We're just trying to make conversation.

FANNY. (*Cheerily.*) You're jealous of our goods, our clothes, our electrical appliances— We want to be liked for what we are.

MILLY. (*Happily.*) But you're just like us.

FANNY. (*Cheerfully pushing Milly toward the door.*) Go home, now. We want to have a conversation about how awful you are.

MILLY. (*Happily.*) Can't we join you?

JACK. (*To Frank and Fanny, cheerfully.*) Go ahead, talk!

FRANK. We want privacy.

FANNY. (*Cheerfully.*) We're putting our feet down: You have to go.

MILLY. (*Pathetically.*) We don't want to!

JACK. (*Sincerely.*) We want to be friends. (*Taking out a wad of bills and handing Frank some of them.*) Have some money.

FRANK. Don't tempt me.

MILLY. We want to stay.

FANNY. (*Earnestly, sympathetically.*) But we don't like you anymore.

JACK. We'll change.

MILLY. We can be nicer. We just haven't been trying.

JACK. But we *will* try.

FANNY. It sounds hopeless.

MILLY. That seems unfair.

FANNY. It's a lost cause.

MILLY. What kind of friends *are* you?

JACK. *We* can be nice.

MILLY. Give us another chance.

FANNY. (*Looking to Frank for his opinion, they decide to give them the benefit of the doubt, to Milly and Jack.*) Well, all right. You go outside, ring, I'll answer, you come in and be nice.

MILLY. (*Exiting, sincerely.*) Thank you, Fanny. We'll be nice; you'll see.

JACK. (*Exiting, cheerfully.*) See you soon.

FANNY. (*Cheerfully.*) Bye. (*Closing door behind them, to Frank.*) You be reading a paper.

FRANK. (*Past tense, annoyedly.*) I read a paper.

FANNY. (*Sitting down with a magazine.*) Read it from another point of view. I'll be reading a ladies' magazine. (*Starting to read the magazine, getting very engrossed, flipping through the pages, Frank reluctantly takes up his newspaper but is too annoyed to actually look at it, Fanny glances up and sees he's not reading it.*) You reading it?

FRANK. (*Irritably.*) All right!—I'll read it. (*They read. The doorbell rings.*)

FANNY. (*Getting up, acting confused.*) Wonder who that could be this time of night. (*Frank looks disgusted at the pretense.*) wonder who it is?

FRANK. (*Disgusted.*) Milly and Jack.

FANNY. (*Going to door.*) This late? Oh, I don't think so! (*Opening door.*) Yes?—Milly and Jack! Frank, you were right!

MILLY. (*Happily.*) Fanny, you look wonderful!

JACK. (*Happily.*) You look great, Frank.

MILLY. Hope you don't mind us dropping in this time of night.

FANNY. (*Cheerfully.*) Not a bit.

FRANK. (*Sullenly.*) I was reading.

MILLY. (*Concerned.*) Did we interrupt you?—I'd rather cut out my tongue!

FRANK. (*Annoyedly.*) Well, I *was* reading.

MILLY. (*Dismayed.*) This is awful! Where's a knife!—I'm cutting out my tongue! What a lovely home! Is it yours?

FANNY. (*Cheerfully, proudly.*) That's right.

MILLY. Love it! It hits just the right note!

JACK. It's great! (*To Frank.*) You know, you look just like you do at work, only more so.

FRANK. (*Happily.*) I'd recognize you anywhere. (*The curtains start to close.*)

JACK. You know, I like you at the office, but here I *really* like you.

FRANK. (*Happily.*) Aw, go on! (*The curtains are closing.*)

JACK. No, I mean it!

FANNY. (*Happily.*) I suppose you want some drinks.

JACK. Right!

FANNY. (*Happily.*) I suppose I have to *fix* the drinks, right?

FRANK. (*Happily.*) Right! Why don't *you* fix them? (*The curtains are nearly closed now.*)

FANNY. (*Getting up, happily.*) As usual, the pleasure's all mine.

MILLY. (*Happily.*) What a charming place to call a home! It's got real potential! (*The curtains are closed entirely.*)

END PLAY

PROPERTY PLOT

On Stage:
  Coffee table. On it:
    Newspaper
    Magazine
    Vase
  Lamp
  Sofa
  Easy chairs (2)
  Portable bar, with liquor bottles, glasses, ice
  Curtains and curtain rod
  Sideboard. In it:
    Deck of cards

Off Stage:
  Pie
  Serving knife, plates, forks
  Bakery box, with cake
  Tray, with:
    Coffee pot
    Sugar bowl
    Creamer
    Cups and saucers
    Spoons
  Card table and chairs

Personal:
  Roll of bills (Jack)

45

NEW PLAYS

★ **AS BEES IN HONEY DROWN by Douglas Carter Beane.** Winner of the John Gassner Playwriting Award. A hot young novelist finds the subject of his new screenplay in a New York socialite who leads him into the world of *Auntie Mame* and *Breakfast at Tiffany's*, before she takes him for a ride. "A delicious soufflé of a satire ... [an] extremely entertaining fable for an age that always chooses image over substance." *–The NY Times* "... A witty assessment of one of the most active and relentless industries in a consumer society ... the creation of 'hot' young things, which the media have learned to mass produce with efficiency and zeal." *–The NY Daily News* [3M, 3W, flexible casting] ISBN: 0-8222-1651-5

★ **STUPID KIDS by John C. Russell.** In rapid, highly stylized scenes, the story follows four high-school students as they make their way from first through eighth period and beyond, struggling with the fears, frustrations, and longings peculiar to youth. "In STUPID KIDS ... playwright John C. Russell gets the opera of adolescence to a T ... The stylized teenspeak of STUPID KIDS ... suggests that Mr. Russell may have hidden a tape recorder under a desk in study hall somewhere and then scoured the tapes for good quotations ... it is the kids' insular, ceaselessly churning world, a pre-adult world of Doritos and libidos, that the playwright seeks to lay bare." *–The NY Times* "STUPID KIDS [is] a sharp-edged ... whoosh of teen angst and conformity anguish. It is also very funny." *–NY Newsday* [2M, 2W] ISBN: 0-8222-1698-1

★ **COLLECTED STORIES by Donald Margulies.** From Obie Award-winner Donald Margulies comes a provocative analysis of a student-teacher relationship that turns sour when the protégé becomes a rival. "With his fine ear for detail, Margulies creates an authentic, insular world, and he gives equal weight to the opposing viewpoints of two formidable characters." *–The LA Times* "This is probably Margulies' best play to date ..." *–The NY Post* "... always fluid and lively, the play is thick with ideas, like a stock-pot of good stew." *–The Village Voice* [2W] ISBN: 0-8222-1640-X

★ **FREEDOMLAND by Amy Freed.** An overdue showdown between a son and his father sets off fireworks that illuminate the neurosis, rage and anxiety of one family – and of America at the turn of the millennium. "FREEDOMLAND's more obvious links are to *Buried Child* and *Bosoms and Neglect*. Freed, like Guare, is an inspired wordsmith with a gift for surreal touches in situations grounded in familiar and real territory." *–Curtain Up* [3M, 4W] ISBN: 0-8222-1719-8

★ **STOP KISS by Diana Son.** A poignant and funny play about the ways, both sudden and slow, that lives can change irrevocably. There's so much that is vital and exciting about STOP KISS ... you want to embrace this young author and cheer her onto other works ... the writing on display here is funny and credible ... you also will be charmed by its heartfelt characters and up-to-the-minute humor." *–The NY Daily News* "... irresistibly exciting ... a sweet, sad, and enchantingly sincere play." *–The NY Times* [3M, 3W] ISBN: 0-8222-1731-7

★ **THREE DAYS OF RAIN by Richard Greenberg.** The sins of fathers and mothers make for a bittersweet elegy in this poignant and revealing drama. "... a work so perfectly judged it heralds the arrival of a major playwright ... Greenberg is extraordinary." *–The NY Daily News* "Greenberg's play is filled with graceful passages that are by turns melancholy, harrowing, and often, quite funny." *–Variety* [2M, 1W] ISBN: 0-8222-1676-0

★ **THE WEIR by Conor McPherson.** In a bar in rural Ireland, the local men swap spooky stories in an attempt to impress a young woman from Dublin who recently moved into a nearby "haunted" house. However, the tables are soon turned when she spins a yarn of her own. "You shed all sense of time at this beautiful and devious new play." *–The NY Times* "Sheer theatrical magic. I have rarely been so convinced that I have just seen a modern classic. Tremendous." *–The London Daily Telegraph* [4M, 1W] ISBN: 0-8222-1706-6

DRAMATISTS PLAY SERVICE, INC.
440 Park Avenue South, New York, NY 10016 212-683-8960 Fax 212-213-1539
postmaster@dramatists.com   www.dramatists.com

NEW PLAYS

★ **CLOSER by Patrick Marber.** Winner of the 1998 Olivier Award for Best Play and the 1999 New York Drama Critics Circle Award for Best Foreign Play. Four lives intertwine over the course of four and a half years in this densely plotted, stinging look at modern love and betrayal. "CLOSER is a sad, savvy, often funny play that casts a steely, unblinking gaze at the world of relationships and lets you come to your own conclusions ... CLOSER does not merely hold your attention; it burrows into you." –*New York Magazine* "A powerful, darkly funny play about the cosmic collision between the sun of love and the comet of desire." –*Newsweek Magazine* [2M, 2W] ISBN: 0-8222-1722-8

★ **THE MOST FABULOUS STORY EVER TOLD by Paul Rudnick.** A stage manager, headset and prompt book at hand, brings the house lights to half, then dark, and cues the creation of the world. Throughout the play, she's in control of everything. In other words, she's either God, or she thinks she is. "Line by line, Mr. Rudnick may be the funniest writer for the stage in the United States today ... One-liners, epigrams, withering put-downs and flashing repartee: These are the candles that Mr. Rudnick lights instead of cursing the darkness ... a testament to the virtues of laughing ... and in laughter, there is something like the memory of Eden." –*The NY Times* "Funny it is ... consistently, rapaciously, deliriously ... easily the funniest play in town." –*Variety* [4M, 5W] ISBN: 0-8222-1720-1

★ **A DOLL'S HOUSE by Henrik Ibsen, adapted by Frank McGuinness.** Winner of the 1997 Tony Award for Best Revival. "New, raw, gut-twisting and gripping. Easily the hottest drama this season." –*USA Today* "Bold, brilliant and alive." –*The Wall Street Journal* "A thunderclap of an evening that takes your breath away." –*Time Magazine* [4M, 4W, 2 boys] ISBN: 0-8222-1636-1

★ **THE HERBAL BED by Peter Whelan.** The play is based on actual events which occurred in Stratford-upon-Avon in the summer of 1613, when William Shakespeare's elder daughter was publicly accused of having a sexual liaison with a married neighbor and family friend. "In his probing new play, THE HERBAL BED ... Peter Whelan muses about a sidelong event in the life of Shakespeare's family and creates a finely textured tapestry of love and lies in the early 17th-century Stratford." –*The NY Times* "It is a first rate drama with interesting moral issues of truth and expediency." –*The NY Post* [5M, 3W] ISBN: 0-8222-1675-2

★ **SNAKEBIT by David Marshall Grant.** A study of modern friendship when put to the test. "... a rather smart and absorbing evening of water-cooler theater, the intimate sort of Off-Broadway experience that has you picking apart the recognizable characters long after the curtain calls." – *The NY Times* "Off-Broadway keeps on presenting us with compelling reasons for going to the theater. The latest is SNAKEBIT, David Marshall Grant's smart new comic drama about being thirtysomething and losing one's way in life." –*The NY Daily News* [3M, 1W] ISBN: 0-8222-1724-4

★ **A QUESTION OF MERCY by David Rabe.** The Obie Award-winning playwright probes the sensitive and controversial issue of doctor-assisted suicide in the age of AIDS in this poignant drama. "There are many devastating ironies in Mr. Rabe's beautifully considered, piercingly clear-eyed work ..." –*The NY Times* "With unsettling candor and disturbing insight, the play arouses pity and understanding of a troubling subject ... Rabe's provocative tale is an affirmation of dignity that rings clear and true." –*Variety* [6M, 1W] ISBN: 0-8222-1643-4

★ **DIMLY PERCEIVED THREATS TO THE SYSTEM by Jon Klein.** Reality and fantasy overlap with hilarious results as this unforgettable family attempts to survive the nineties. "Here's a play whose point about fractured families goes to the heart, mind – and ears." –*The Washington Post* "... an end-of-the millennium comedy about a family on the verge of a nervous breakdown ... Trenchant and hilarious ..." –*The Baltimore Sun* [2M, 4W] ISBN: 0-8222-1677-9

DRAMATISTS PLAY SERVICE, INC.
440 Park Avenue South, New York, NY 10016 212-683-8960 Fax 212-213-1539
postmaster@dramatists.com www.dramatists.com

NEW PLAYS

★ **HONOUR by Joanna Murray-Smith.** In a series of intense confrontations, a wife, husband, lover and daughter negotiate the forces of passion, history, responsibility and honour. "HONOUR makes for surprisingly interesting viewing. Tight, crackling dialogue (usually played out in punchy verbal duels) captures characters unable to deal with emotions ... Murray-Smith effectively places her characters in situations that strip away pretense." –*Variety* "... the play's virtues are strong: a distinctive theatrical voice, passionate concerns ... HONOUR might just capture a few honors of its own." –*Time Out Magazine* [1M, 3W] ISBN: 0-8222-1683-3

★ **MR. PETERS' CONNECTIONS by Arthur Miller.** Mr. Miller describes the protagonist as existing in a dream-like state when the mind is "freed to roam from real memories to conjectures, from trivialities to tragic insights, from terror of death to glorying in one's being alive." With this memory play, the Tony Award and Pulitzer Prize-winner reaffirms his stature as the world's foremost dramatist. "... a cross between Joycean stream-of-consciousness and Strindberg's dream plays, sweetened with a dose of William Saroyan's philosophical whimsy ... CONNECTIONS is most intriguing ..." –*The NY Times* [5M, 3W] ISBN: 0-8222-1687-6

★ **THE WAITING ROOM by Lisa Loomer.** Three women from different centuries meet in a doctor's waiting room in this dark comedy about the timeless quest for beauty – and its cost. "... THE WAITING ROOM ... is a bold, risky melange of conflicting elements that is ... terrifically moving ... There's no resisting the fierce emotional pull of the play." –*The NY Times* "... one of the high points of this year's Off-Broadway season ... THE WAITING ROOM is well worth a visit." –*Back Stage* [7M, 4W, flexible casting] ISBN: 0-8222-1594-2

★ **THE OLD SETTLER by John Henry Redwood.** A sweet-natured comedy about two church-going sisters in 1943 Harlem and the handsome young man who rents a room in their apartment. "For all of its decent sentiments, THE OLD SETTLER avoids sentimentality. It has the authenticity and lack of pretense of an Early American sampler." –*The NY Times* "We've had some fine plays Off-Broadway this season, and this is one of the best." –*The NY Post* [1M, 3W] ISBN: 0-8-222-1642-6

★ **THE LAST TRAIN TO NIBROC by Arlene Hutton.** In 1940 two young strangers share a seat on a train bound east only to find their paths will cross again. "All aboard. LAST TRAIN TO NIBROC is a sweetly told little chamber romance." –*Show Business* "... [a] gently charming little play, reminiscent of Thorton Wilder in its look at rustic Americans who are to be treasured for their simplicity and directness ..." *Associated Press* "The old formula of boy wins girl, boy loses girl, boy wins girl still works ... [a] well-made play that perfectly captures a slice of small-town-life-gone-by." –*Back Stage* [1M, 1W] ISBN: 0-8222-1753-8

★ **OVER THE RIVER AND THROUGH THE WOODS by Joe DiPietro.** Nick sees both sets of his grandparents every Sunday for dinner. This is routine until he has to tell them that he's been offered a dream job in Seattle. The news doesn't sit so well. "A hilarious family comedy that is even funnier than his long running musical revue *I Love You, You're Perfect, Now Change*." –*Back Stage* "Loaded with laughs every step of the way." –*Star-Ledger* [3M, 3W] ISBN: 0-8222-1712-0

★ **SIDE MAN by Warren Leight.** 1999 Tony Award winner. This is the story of a broken family and the decline of jazz as popular entertainment. "... a tender, deeply personal memory play about the turmoil in the family of a jazz musician as his career crumbles at the dawn of the age of rock-and-roll ..." –*The NY Times* "[SIDE MAN] is an elegy for two things – a lost world and a lost love. When the two notes sound together in harmony, it is moving and graceful ..." –*The NY Daily News* "An atmospheric memory play...with crisp dialogue and clearly drawn characters ... reflects the passing of an era with persuasive insight ... The joy and despair of the musicians is skillfully illustrated." –*Variety* [5M, 3W] ISBN: 0-8222-1721-X

DRAMATISTS PLAY SERVICE, INC.
440 Park Avenue South, New York, NY 10016 212-683-8960 Fax 212-213-1539
postmaster@dramatists.com   www.dramatists.com